Nkosi sikelel' iAfrik

nakanyisw' uphondo

zwa imithandazo yet

Nkosi sikelela

Thina lusapho lwayo

na boloka setjhaba sa

e dintwa le matshwe

e, O se boloke setjha

a South Afrika – Sou

FLYING WITH PRIDE

the story of the south african flag

published by

WildNet Africa

www.WildNetAfrica.com

Published by WildNet Africa (Pty) Ltd.

WildNet Africa (Pty) Ltd.
Box 73528 Lynnwood Ridge 0040
Pretoria South Africa
www.WildNetAfrica.com

Concept: Andrew McKenzie
Project management: WildNet Africa project team
Design & layout: Penny Waterkeyn
Text: Denis Beckett
Production: Andre du Preez

Printed with Pride in South Africa by Formeset Printers.
Flying with Pride: The Story of the South African Flag. Text by Denis Beckett.
p. cm.
Includes flag information, drawing instructions, coat of arms and text.

ISBN 0 - 620 - 28903 - 1

FLYING WITH PRIDE LIVES AND GROWS FOREVER...

www.FlyingWithPride.co.za

BENEFICIARIES

WILD FOUNDATION SA

The WILD Foundation SA - formerly the Wilderness Foundation founded by Dr Ian Player in 1972 - is dedicated to advocating the protection of wilderness and wild lands of southern Africa, and the understanding of indigenous culture. It works to achieve this by public awareness campaigns and meetings, by promoting wilderness as a resource for all South Africans through experiential and educational programs and by monitoring and assisting with the management of existing and potential wilderness areas under both private and public ownership.

Wild.org

GONDWANA ALIVE SOCIETY

The Gondwana Alive Society seeks to assemble and spread the relevant knowledge, canvas a critical mass of concerned opinion and sustain action through coming decades, all of this towards "Promoting biodiversity and stemming the Sixth Extinction". One of the aims of Gondwana Alive is to reach every school in former Gondwanaland with the message that something can be done to halt the inexorable decline of the planet brought about by man's activities. This effort starts at the individual level, but is multiplied by a unified concept of common destiny.

GondwanaAlive.org

MARETLWANE BUSHVELD SCHOOL

The Pretoria Boys High School's bushveld school and outreach programme, Maretlwane, is situated in the protected heart of the Magaliesberg Mountains near Pretoria, South Africa. The rocks are as ancient as any on Earth; the water is unsullied. There the pupils can sit in silence while the Earth speaks to them. Maretlwane aspires to act as a model of how people can most effectively make a difference to the environment by starting close to home, and of how communities, via their schools, can acknowledge and enhance the role and importance of wilderness in modern society.

Maretlwane.net

PUBLISHER'S NOTE

Nobody living in South Africa at the time of transition could have helped noticing how one thing rose above all others and has remained there, unassailed, ever since. In the literal sense this was the new, colourful, by now quite famous, South African flag. Figuratively too, when the chips were down, it was the flag; a unifying force when things threatened to tear us apart.

The idea of publishing *Flying with Pride* arose after reflecting upon the many ways in which the flag had become integrated into the very fabric of our new society. It had become key rings and playing cards. It had become rulers and ties, and shirts and hats, and belts and shoes and ... so much more.

But besides the obvious trinkets and gear, it had also become part of our image of ourselves. It had become logos and icons for anything from a two-person business to a huge corporation, from a township project to a Government Department. It had morphed into the Welcome Man, and from there into an umbrella. It had become a flower, a golfer, a tree and a diamond. It flowed and it ran, it flew and it swam. Where it wasn't the flag itself, it was the colours of the flag, subtly woven into a pattern or texture, stopping one short in the traffic as the colours suddenly leapt out as something hugely more.

In short, as *Flying with Pride* shows, the South African flag has been used in a greater variety of ways than any other flag in the world. And the huge significance of this? Simply that the adoption of our flag as a symbol unity is something that each and every one of us has done. We, the ordinary people, have triumphed. And in that we have something of which we can be truly proud.

Our flag is part of our heritage, and of our make-up. So too is our environment. For this reason WildNet Africa has donated the proceeds of *Flying with Pride* to custodians of that heritage in the knowledge that without heritage, both cultural and environmental, we are but nothing.

Andrew McKenzie
Founder and Director: WildNet Africa
Pretoria, April 2002

FOREWORD

It was difficult to imagine, back then in the days of negotiations, that this assortment of shapes and colours we had before us would become such a central part of defining and identifying a new nation. Indeed, it took some effort to even recognise that what we had on paper could actually become a flag, something we would be prepared to raise outside a democratic parliament.

The route to a new South African flag, which could at once represent the values of a new society and unite all the people of the country around them, was not an easy one. The obstacles were many and great – a country which had been at war with itself a mere few years before, decades of suspicion and fear, vastly differing expectations and views of a new constitutional order.

There were smaller obstacles too. On the afternoon, during the pre-election negotiations, when we needed to make a decision on the new flag, the ANC team was presented with a problem – its president, Nelson Mandela, was away in Rustenburg. There was no question of proceeding without his approval. There was also no time to take a copy of the proposed flag to him. So, calling on the same resourcefulness which had helped to unblock the negotiation process several times before, we faxed a drawing of the flag to him and got someone in Rustenburg to colour in the various shapes with the appropriate colours. And thus the flag of a new South Africa – on a sheet of fax paper, coloured by hand – was approved by the person who was to become its first democratically elected president.

The design of the new flag was unveiled to a waiting South Africa. Some praised it. Others thought it brash and garish. Yet, as it was raised on flagpoles across the country in the first minutes of Wednesday, 27 April 1994, few could fail to recognise that it symbolised a new dawn for a nation that had spent so many years in darkness. Since then South Africa has adopted a final democratic constitution, has twice elected its public representatives at all levels of government, has established democratic institutions, has undertaken a difficult, yet earnest, process of uncovering the truth of its past and laying a basis for reconciliation, has begun the process of meeting the most basic needs of its people and has established its rightful place within the global community of nations.

As South Africa has taken these giant steps towards a better future, it has done so united under the flag of a democratic nation and committed to the values which it represents. As South Africans daily work to build a better society, they are surrounded in many forms and countless manifestations by a flag which recognises and celebrates the unity and diversity of the country's people.

Few would have imagined almost a decade ago that this collection of colourful shapes could become such a potent symbol of unity and progress. But then fewer still would have thought that a country torn apart by decades of racial oppression could transform itself into a beacon of democracy and hope.

It is a testament to the determination and far-sightedness of its people that today South Africa is free – and that the bright, optimistic flag of a new nation flies across the country and across the world.

Cyril Ramaphosa
Johannesburg, April 2002

ACKNOWLEDGEMENTS

Many individuals and organisations contributed of their time, energy and resources in taking *Flying with Pride* from concept to reality. The publishers would like to thank Fred Brownell, former State Herald, for his boundless enthusiasm, sage advice and access to his collection of articles and artefacts related to the flag.

Colonel Neil Thomas and all the staff at the SAAF Museum are thanked for hosting South Africa's first Flag Carnival held at Swartkops Airforce Base, and Kim Helfrich for going that extra mile.

We thank our sponsors and donors elsewhere on these pages for their assistance in creating awareness and reducing the cost of publication of *Flying with Pride*, thereby increasing the revenue raised for the beneficiaries.

To the children from across South Africa who entered the *Flying with Pride* art competition we are especially grateful. Their works appear in the body of the book, in a special section at the back, and on the FlyingWithPride.co.za website in perpetuity.

From across the world people submitted pictures, anecdotes and suggestions for *Flying with Pride*, while back home the staff and families of WildNet Africa made considerable sacrifices in bringing the book to life in what were trying times: a fitting tribute to their enthusiastic participation in WildNet Africa's support for heritage-related organisations and initiatives.

Of the many individuals who helped we would especially like to thank Penny Waterkeyn, who went far beyond the call of duty as designer, as well as Annamarie Roux, Andre du Preez and Dr Jack the cartoonist.

DONORS

Beeld — beeld.com
Sunday Times — sundaytimes.co.za
The Star — star.co.za
Pretoria News — pretorianews.co.za
PictureNET Africa — picturenet.co.za
Gallo Images — gallo-images.co.za
Touchline Photo — touchline.co.za
Thompsons South Africa Tours & Travel — thompsons.co.za
Voetsek! — voetsek.co.uk

SUBSCRIBERS

Aan de Vliet   Nic and Sue Adams   Alan Ainslie   Daryl Balfour   Andrew Bannister   Gary Bernard   Don Boroughs
John E. Bryan   Dr. Jeremy Cripps   Siddique Davids   De Wildt Cheetah Centre   Die Werf   Duif Du Toit   Dennis Farrell   Henner Frankenfeld
The Gilbrides   Government Communications and Information Systems Library   Wayne Griffiths   David Guttenfeldder   Themba Hadebe
Advocate H.F. Junod & Family   Kapama Private Game Reserve   Sasa Kralj   Lakenvlei Forest Lodge   Luc Hosten   Magoebaskloof Hotel
Motorsport SA   Mount Grace Hotel   Eddie Mtsweni   Grant Murdoch   Palesa   Tertius Pickard   Jacques Pieterse   Pondoro Game Reserve
Gary Prior   David Rogers   Russel Friedman Books   SA Flyer   SA National Skydiving Team   Rodney Schick   The Elephant Sanctuary
The E-mail Corporation   The Green Catering Company   THOS - The House of Synergy   The Ranch Hotel   The SA Business Club
Thulamela Guest House   Varsity Bakery   The Weidemann Family   Colin Whelan   WildlifeDecisionSupport.com

FUNCTION SPONSORS

Ster-Kinekor Theatres — sterkinekor.com
Cape Town Tourism — cape-town.org
Sheraton Pretoria Hotel & Towers — sheraton.com
SAAF Museum — saafmuseum.co.za

PUBLICITY PARTNERS OF FLYING WITH PRIDE

DE BEERS

A DIAMOND IS FOREVER

and

PROUDLY SOUTH AFRICAN

Eskom

SOUTH AFRICAN AIRWAYS

SABC

OLD MUTUAL

Telkom

Proudly South African Founder Sponsors

FLYING WITH PRIDE

For those who give strength through faith in others.
Let the pride in.

THE RIVER SWELLS from the little streams.

- African proverb -

Mugabe has 2-thirds
26 nuwe belastings

March 1994 was an exciting month, all right, with a new nation about to be born. But there were jitters too, big-league jitters.

WOULD THE ARMY MUTINY? WOULD THE RIGHT-WING STAGE A PUTSCH? WOULD INKATHA UNLEASH IMPIS? AND – SHUDDER – WHAT IF JUST ONE RANDOM ASSASSIN GOT AT EITHER OF THE FIGURES ON THE CENTRE STAGE, FW DE KLERK OR NELSON

March was not restful on the nerves. It didn't help that in the middle of the month the media showed us a strange, multi-coloured cloth and told us that this was our new national flag.

South Africans were not that massively inclined to welcome a new flag. The preceding year had seen a whole stack of would-be flags offered for public scrutiny. All were brutally howled down. Now came this new one, and no-one was asking us "hey, people, what do you think?" They were simply saying "here's your flag."

SOUTH AFRICANS WERE NOT THAT MASSIVELY INCLINED TO WELCOME A NEW FLAG.

Some people, including the more timorously inclined of every political hue, were not at all keen on any new flag. Why taunt the guys who were already growling? The growlers had plenty of wreckage capacity. They were giving up their claim to rule; let them have their bit of bunting. Most countries in the world had at some stage extended their franchise from the few to the many, and hardly any had felt the need to change the flag (unless they were simultaneously acquiring independence). What extravagance, too, in a country rife with poverty. And look at the thing! A jumble of colour, like a box for a children's cereal or a soap-powder.

There was a spate of public commentary, most of it uncomplimentary. Funny, someone remarked, the flag was supposed to unite South Africa and so it did.

Everyone disliked it.

Then the flag virtually vanished from view. We had other

VOLKSTAAAAT..
NUWE SA
ANDERO VOSLOO
27.4.94

things to worry about in the run-up to the election. The social thermometer was on a roller-coaster, with question-marks over who was participating, who was boycotting, and whether ballot or bullet would prevail on election day. Every news bulletin brought new hope or new fear or a bit of both.

By the closing days, the thermometer had dropped from red alert. The Inkatha Freedom Party was in, at last, and each of the disgruntled edges of the spectrum – Afrikaner Right and Africanist Left – had at least one party participating. Still, the election hung on a knife-edge, and early on April 27 fate seemed to favour the wrong side of the knife.

THIS WAS NOT A DAY THAT HATE WAS GOING TO WIN. THIS WAS A DAY THAT UNITY HAD WON.

The news was ominous. Item one: bomb attack in Johannesburg. Item two: bomb blast in Burgersdorp. Marrows chilled in the autumn morning. If this was the day's start, what lay before its end? Landmines at the polls? Gunbattles in the streets? The social temperature was back in the danger zone.

But as the day warmed, a benign wind blew through minds and souls. The bomb-blast count went not up but down; Burgersdorp, repeatedly announced in the early morning, evaporated as a hoax. Everybody saw the TV scenes: long, patient, peaceful queues snaking through veld and parks and playing-fields. Nearly everybody stood in one, shoulder to shoulder with nearly everybody else. We knew in our bones that South Africa had passed the hump. This was not a day that hate was going to win. This was a day that unity had won.

Farmer and labourer, maid and madam, manager and unionist, greeted and shared sun-shades and chatted. We loved, that day. We loved our compatriots in a way we had never done before, in a way we so far haven't quite managed to do again. We queued as equals and as friends. Parties and politics were secondary as we shared a common relief. All our lives we'd assumed that an apocalyptic clash lay in wait. And here we stood in the extraordinary ordinariness of long, lovely queues, seeing that clash evaporate before our very eyes. Worry was a thing for another day. For this day, we glowed.

And we talked. We suspended the rules – about introductions, about social classes, about compatibility... We talked to the person in front, we talked to the person behind, we talked to the people two away, and in the most jammed and static of queues there were wholesale mass tea-parties. Only thing is, we often didn't have that much to say.

Except for one instant, ready-made subject.

There, flying over the polling station, was this novel feature

of our reborn collective life. There was the new national flag which had been hoisted officially, nation-wide, that morning. This was the first time nearly anyone saw it in real life, and what a talking point it made. It was extremely central to the occasion, after all, and it was not a sectional thing. This was everybody's flag. Everybody had sight of it – often several hours of uninterrupted sight – and everybody had a view on it, a view unaffected by race or age or gender or income.

The green should be narrower. There should be less blue and red, with more yellow. The blue must be on top, the sky is blue. No, the red must be on top, the newspaper said so. It's not yellow, it's gold. It's not red, it's dark orange.

It was the best kind of argument – without acrimony, with no "you people..." and "your kind...". Best of all, though, was the way we wore in as the day wore on.

By sundown we were a different country to the one we had been at sun-up. The starkest difference lay in the flag, and our attitudes to it.

Even in the morning, comments had advanced from the

AND SO IT BEGAN *The release of Nelson Mandela from prison in 1990 set in motion a process which culminated in a new dispensation, and a new flag, for South Africa.*

"oh, no" flavour that the media reported in March. It was as if now that people knew the flag in person, as it were, they were politer to it than when it was a mere television celebrity. But by the evening comments were not just polite. They were heartfelt. This day had been so fulfilling, and the flag had been so big a part of it. Wellbeing brimmed through every sense, with this multi-coloured cloth as its symbol. At a Soweto polling station a young woman said "Until yesterday I felt that the old flag was my nation's flag. But this one, I love." That struck a chord.

April 27 1994 was South Africa's moment of elation. On a glorious day a fortnight later, the moment was consolidated. An immensely dignified man in a dark suit stood under a canopy in front of the Union Buildings. Installed in an office he had once sought to destroy, he received the salutes of soldiers who had once sought to destroy him. We the people clustered as one around our television screens. For a second time, fears and worries took time off. We differed, that day, in little but the materials we used to clear the mists of emotion – handkerchiefs or sleeves, tissues or the backs of our hands. When the helicopters flew past, giving the now less-strange flag an airing like no flag had ever seen, we were high on pride and relief and confidence.

THIS DAY HAD BEEN SO FULFILLING,
AND THE FLAG HAD BEEN SO BIG A PART OF IT.

By the evening of that momentous day – Inauguration Day, May 10 1994 – the thermometer of South Africa's threats and conflicts was as low as it had ever been. It was a time of triumph. We were large, we wrought miracles, we could do anything. Perhaps no-one who hadn't lived through the years beforehand would ever know the feeling. The allegedly inevitable meeting of irresistible force and immovable

object had filled us with daunting images of fights to the last. Now it was gone. We had danced our way through it, surprising ourselves and astonishing the world.

But... was it a Fools' Honeymoon? Beneath the exuberant surface, doubts gnawed. Mere weeks before, the forces of resistance had loomed like a dark spectre. They now seemed to have calmly marched off to oblivion, as if the hardliners decided that they would do better to argue from within than to batter the walls from without. That would be truly miraculous. But it verged on being too miraculous to believe. I found my answer in a bar in Mitchell Street, Pretoria West, two months later. I found it because of a present from my wife.

After the inauguration, my wife made me a tie. She made it by hand with strips of ribbon, in the colours of the flag.

Suddenly I discovered all sorts of occasions to wear a tie, and my wife's sewing was put to the test. At close quarters, the sight of the nation's flag hanging on a person's neck was dazzling, and I became used to exclamations. And to

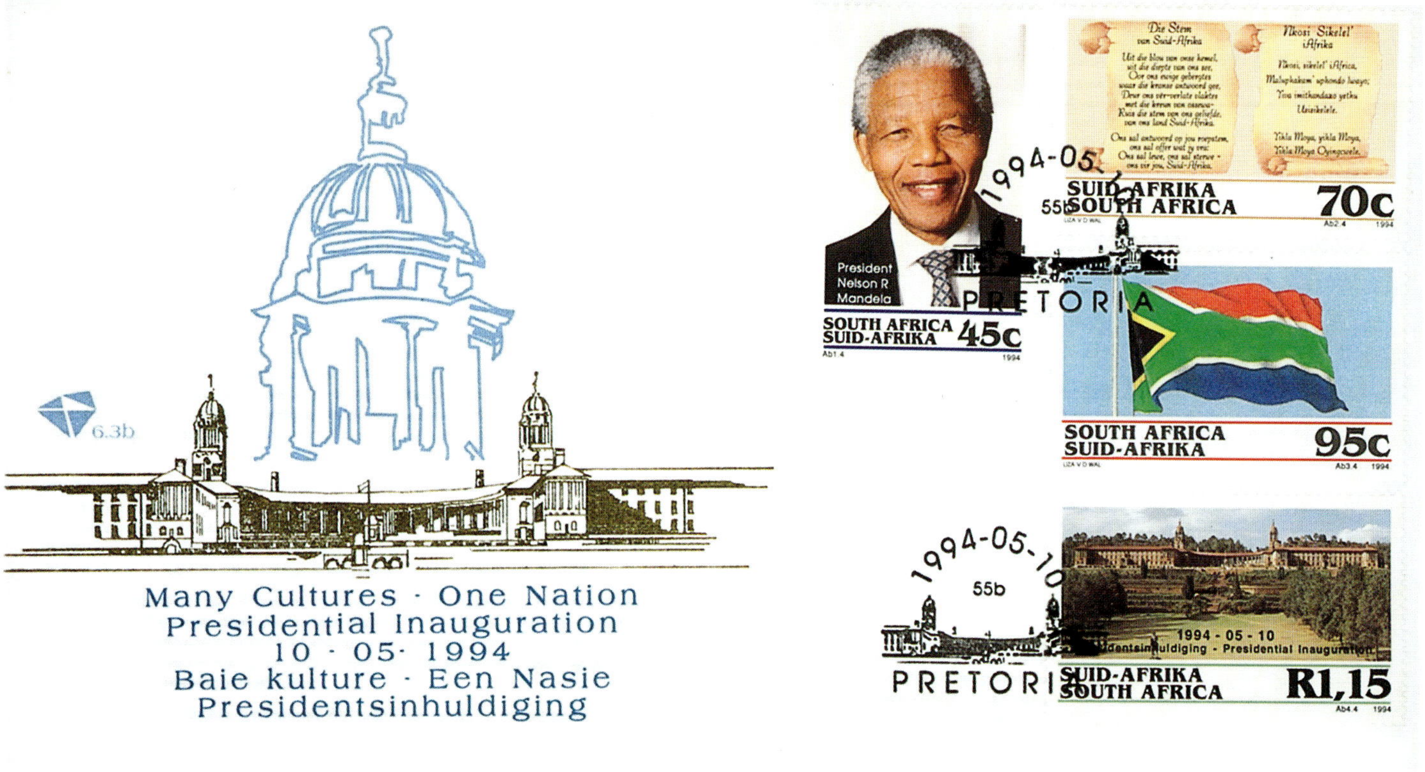
6.3b
Many Cultures · One Nation
Presidential Inauguration
10 · 05 · 1994
Baie kulture · Een Nasie
Presidentsinhuldiging
President Nelson R Mandela
SOUTH AFRICA SUID-AFRIKA 45c
SUID-AFRIKA SOUTH AFRICA 70c
SOUTH AFRICA SUID-AFRIKA 95c
SUID-AFRIKA SOUTH AFRICA R1,15
1994-05-10
55b
PRETORIA

curious fingers wishing to explore the texture. And to offers, requests and pleas, often running to hundreds of rands if I would sell on the spot.

But a bar in Mitchell Street... that might be different. This is Pretoria West, note. We're not talking smooth, larney eastern Pretoria, where people have degrees on their walls and shop assistants address you in English. Pretoria West is industrial territory, tattoo territory, tough territory.

I was on my way from a formal function, dressed in suit and tie. The tie. It was lunchtime, and I had stopped for a beer and a steak. I walked into the public bar. It was crowded. I had an instant impression of two-day stubble, short-sleeve overalls, and huge hairy rippling arms, holding beers. Slightly less instantly, I began to feel like a goldfish in a bowl. These large guys with their hard faces were turning and looking. Looking my way. I didn't understand. I'd previously known times as the *langharige Engelse liberalis*, uncertainly welcome, but hey, we'd moved on.

That stuff was old history now, wasn't it?

Then I clicked. I was wearing the flag! In a public bar in Pretoria West. This was perhaps not tactful, here in the heartland of the old South Africa. But I was in it now, whatever the cost. This was my flag, I was proud of it. They didn't have to like it, any more than I had to like their tattoos.

I tried to talk my pulse-rate down to normality, but it wasn't wholly convinced. Especially not when two large guys detached themselves from a group – the group that had done the closest staring and peering – and manoeuvred their way in my direction. I noticed, with a downward lurch of the confidence index, that one guy seemed to have walked out of a street-fight movie. He had scars all over and a fist so large that the quart it was clutching looked like a dumpy.

The two come up close. Very close. Too close. I feel a thicket of butterflies aflutter in my stomach. Then the street-fight guy speaks. I'm pretending I haven't noticed, but my nerves are very aware that he is opening his mouth

to address me. He says: *"Ag meneer verskoon, sê my asseblief waar kry ons so 'n das?"*

For a moment, I can't believe it. I'm expecting abuse and I get "excuse me sir". I'm picturing the tie as a red rag to a bull, and I get a customer. I burst out laughing. Not least, I'm laughing in the privilege of living in so invigorating a land. How very much stability and repose and predictability I am willing to sacrifice for the voyage of human discovery.

THROUGH IT ALL, THE FLAG FLEW, UNASSAILED, UNDILUTED, OWNED EQUALLY BY US ALL ...

In no time I'm sitting with Schalk and Corrie and their pals, and more beer is sliding down the gullet than I had intended. The afternoon soon vanishes and I finally must take a very long walk before I resume the driver's seat. I have also been abundantly apprised that these guys are by no means apostles of liberal brotherhood. Far from it. All they have done is to embrace the reality of the new, but that they have done that is a marvel. "It is *mos* also our country" says somebody when, on Beer Four, we get around to why they'd asked. For some of his pals, the appeal is different; *"Dit lyk blerrie* stylish, *jy weet"* says one.

In the months and years that followed, the nation resumed its regular rocky ride. We had binding moments, to be sure. We also had absolutely no shortage of disappointments, disillusions, finger-pointings and recriminations, with that sad and primitive race fixation lurking below the surface. Even the anthem, sensitively composed to unify South Africans, encountered rocks, with a tendency in some quarters to skip out the "other side's" bits.

Through it all, the flag flew, unassailed, undiluted, owned equally by us all, unique and proud as a symbol of the Rainbow Nation.

Years on, many South Africans forget that we have much to celebrate. We may not have found utopia, but we have acquired a solid foundation. A lot of building lies ahead.

We could do well, as we build, to revel a little in what has already been done. We may benefit from a reminder that great challenges, when met, deliver great rewards. We may take heart from a salute to that cloth of many colours which enfolds so much of our hope.

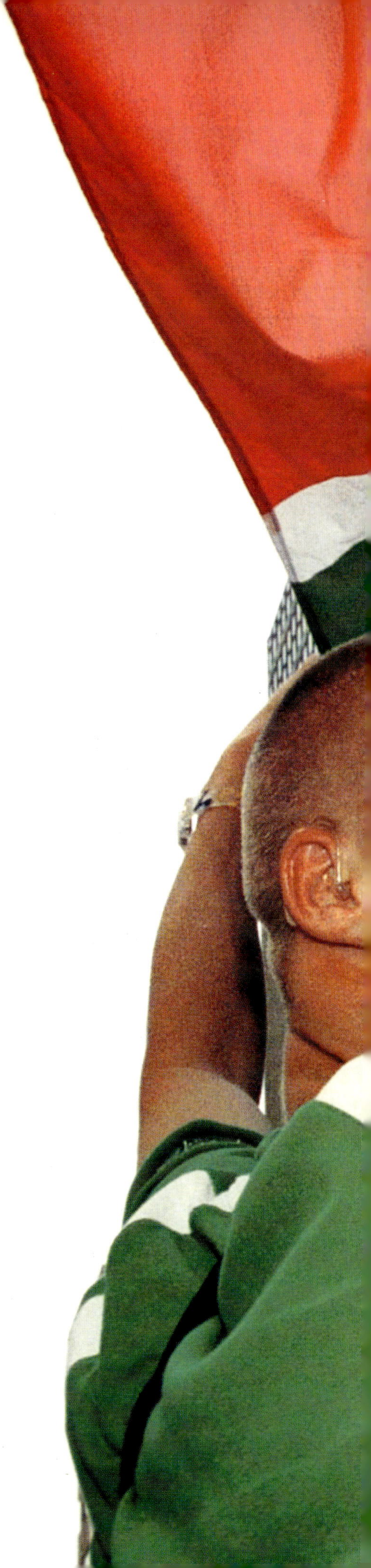

"OUR DEEPEST FEAR IS NOT THAT WE ARE INADEQUATE. Our deepest fear is that we are powerful beyond measure. It is our light, not our darkness, that most frightens us. We ask ourselves, who am I to be brilliant, gorgeous, talented, and fabulous? Actually, who are you not to be? You are a child of God. Your playing small doesn't serve the world. There is nothing enlightened about shrinking so that other people will not feel insecure around you. We were born to manifest the glory of God that is within us. It isn't just some of us, it is everyone And as we let our own light shine, we unconsciously give others permission to do the same. As we are liberated from out own fear, our presence automatically liberates others." – *Nelson Mandela*

NORWICH
37

IF THE RHYTHM OF THE DRUM BEAT CHANGES,
the dance step must adapt.
- African proverb -

NATIONAL YOUTH DAY
EDDIES

HISTORY IS NOT MADE or experienced by Man, but by men, women and children.

- Guy Butler -

When Jan van Riebeeck arrived at the Cape of Good Hope in 1652, a flag came with him.

THAT MUCH IS KNOWN. IT IS ALSO KNOWN THAT THE FLAG WAS A LOT LIKE THE NETHERLANDS FLAG – THREE HORIZONTAL STRIPES, MIDDLE STRIPE WHITE AND BOTTOM STRIPE BLUE. AND THAT IS WHERE WHAT IS KNOWN COMES TO AN END.

Leaving aside the debate about what letters, if any, were shown on the flag[1], no-one knows with certainty what colour the top stripe was. It may have been orange, or it may have been red, or it may have been a colour now called "chilli red", which is halfway between orange and red. Some say "obviously, orange" in honour of the House of Orange. But it's not obvious: there is much evidence for red.

Anyway, the Cape flag may not have been the same. Van Riebeeck did not work for the Netherlands government. He worked for the Dutch East India Company, which was the most powerful company in the world at the time, virtually a State on its own, and had no qualms about expressing symbols of independence.

Then again, the confusion may be not so much about intentions as about dyes. The Bureau of Standards was not yet in business, and the top stripe in practice may have been all three colours – orange, red and chilli – varying from one flag to the other according either to the flag-maker's dye or to the age of the flag. White remained white, until it got dirty. A faded blue remained blue, albeit a lighter blue. But a faded red became an orange. Perhaps the sun in Africa turned red to orange faster than it did in Europe for, by the time the British arrived and changed the Cape's flag to an altogether different pattern of red-white-and-blue, the Cape flag had become known as the "oranje-blanje-blaauw". Meantime the Netherlands had settled on a distinctly red top stripe, which remains to this day.

When the Voortrekkers left the Cape to seek their freedom they answered the twin heritage of red and orange in different ways. The new Transvaal Republic stuck to the Netherlands pattern, with a distinctly red top stripe, but added a green vertical stripe down the left side. Their flag

[1] Possibly VOC, for Vereenigde Oost-Indische Compagnie, the logo under which the Dutch East India Company ruled much of southern Asia. Possibly VOCC, the extra C for "Cabo", Cape. Possibly none.

became widely known as the Vierkleur. The Orange Free State went orange in a big way: their flag was orange and white stripes, with a little Netherlands flag in the corner. The Union of South Africa was born on May 31, 1910. Its birthright included three flags – the Vierkleur, the Free State flag, which never acquired a nickname, and the flag with the most entrenched nickname in history, the Union Jack. Natal and the Cape Province had been British colonies, flying the flag of the empire upon which, at the time, the sun never set[2].

THUS WHEN THE UNION OF SOUTH AFRICA WAS BORN ... THERE WAS NO DEBATE ABOUT THE FLAG.

In 1910, the people of all these provinces became South Africans. The word did not trip lightly off the tongue. What was this thing South Africa? People saw themselves as Transvalers, as Kapenaars, as Pedi, Boer, Xhosa, Venda, British, or the like. Nobody said "I am a South African." It was as if, say, today's Zambia, Malawi, Zimbabwe, Angola, South Africa & Co were to merge as the Republic of Sub-Sahara. We would not instantly adjust to calling ourselves "Sub-Saharans".

Moreover, all were now "British subjects". This was news to many, and not necessarily welcome news. The Boers had put effort into trekking out of stepmother England's reach, and now here was stepmother catching up with them again and giving them her flag to wave. The Afrikaners of Natal and the Cape had been British subjects for decades, but not notably enthusiastic subjects. And of course, this being 1910, nobody in power had asked dark people for their view.

Thus when the Union of South Africa was born, as eclectic a nation as was ever assembled under one flag, there was no debate about the flag. Britannia ruled. Barely six months later, though, voices began to say "Hey, hang on, if we're our own nation now why don't we have our own flag."

On December 9 1910 the Governor-General asked for guidance. He cabled the Secretary of State for the Colonies in Whitehall, London. Guidance came, would you believe, the very next day. The civil servants of great-grandad's day didn't let the in-tray flow over it seems. What Whitehall said was: "...the proper national flag to be flown on land by every citizen of the Empire is the Union Jack, which, in the opinion of His Majesty's Government, should be regarded as the national flag of South Africa..."

Which seemed fairly categorical. However, note that odd phrase "...to be flown on land...". Isn't on land the obvious place to fly a flag? Well, no. In those days the flags you flew at sea were a very big thing. (Flag or no flag, you knew whose land you were on but not whose ship was sailing into your harbour). And this flag, the "ensign", was subject to different rules.

On December 28, not three weeks after the enquiry, the Lords Commissioner of His Majesty's Admiralty gave permission for the South African ensign to be "defaced" (a technical term, derived long before a ring of vandalism crept in) by adding the Armorial Bearings of the Union to the centre.

The "Armorial Bearings" meant a quartered shield carrying the symbol of each province – a young woman holding an anchor; two wildebeest; an orange tree; and an oxwagon. This felt familiar; this was unique and homegrown. But now people began to treat the ensign as their national flag. The government found itself in the awkward position of

2 For which, Ghandi's explanation was: "God can't trust the English in the dark."

PREVIOUS SOUTH AFRICAN FLAGS

The Union Jack (top); The South African Red Ensign (centre); The first national flag of South Africa (below).

"discouraging" the use on land of the flag that its ships officially flew at sea, and was not very successful. Many South Africans, and not only non-English ones, appreciated the symbol of a more distinctive identity than just another outpost of Britain.

However, this more distinctive identity was only a li-i-ttle bit more distinctive. At the best of times you needed 20/20 vision to make out a wagon and wildebeest there in the middle of this background of Britishness. From a distance, the shield was just a blob.

Voices of protest grew fiercer as memories of war and defeat grew dimmer. In 1926 Dr DF Malan (who would later be the first Nationalist Prime Minister) proposed that South Africa acquire its own full-scale flag and abolish the Union Jack altogether. He made his case rather emphatically – "A flag is not a mere cloth. A flag is able to move to tears, stir the deepest springs of action, and inspire to the noblest efforts." But of course the fervour with which he wanted the British symbol gone was no greater than the fervour with which many other South Africans wanted it to stay.

An argument about a cloth, even if not a "mere" cloth, is bound to start off in storm-in-a-teacup mode. Early on General Smuts, leader of the opposition, dismissed it as "screaming farce" and "sorry melodrama". But then the heat built up, so far up that for a while a third Anglo-Boer War seemed on the way. So did rebellion, in quarters such as the Bo-Kaap in Cape Town where people with no British heritage and debatable benefit of the British legacy rioted in defence of the British flag. After nearly two years (during which Smuts' view altered to "this flag calamity threatens to engulf everything") compromise was struck. Forgotten though it is now, the compromise packed an uncommon clout in respect of the might-have-beens of history. Consider that knife-edge again. It was by a knife-edge that South Africa went to war, on Britain's side, eleven years later.

"A FLAG IS NOT A MERE CLOTH.
A FLAG IS ABLE TO MOVE TO TEARS..."

It was by a knife-edge that Hitler was defeated in North Africa. We'll never know what might have happened had Afrikanerdom's deepest springs of action still been burning in resentment at the cloth that stirs.

In terms of square inches, the compromise was more than a trifle lopsided. The Empire and its loyalists swallowed the return of the oranje-blanje-blaauw (this time with an unequivocally orange top bar) at the price of keeping a minuscule Union Jack in its middle, like the armorial bearings had been in the middle of the ensign. The Nationalists in turn insisted on diluting the Union Jack by having the Vierkleur and the Free State flag in there too. The outcome bequeathed the nation's flag-makers with decades of painstaking intricacy.

Since the flag was officially supposed to be flown alongside the Union Jack, the Nationalist side complained that they now had two Union Jacks to salute. The Empire side said they needed a magnifying glass to find their flag in the central clutter. No-one was delighted, no-one was defeated; it was a classic case of compromise. After its unofficial maiden hoisting on March 28 1928 – ironically at a conference on emigration in Havana, Cuba – the flag went forth into a surprisingly placid career lasting just short of the biblical threescore years and ten.

... WHAT THE FLAG FLEW OVER WAS BY NO MEANS PLACID ...

What the flag flew over was by no means placid, but the flag itself was never a major focus of attack, whether in campus protests or revolutionary rhetoric. There was always a degree of ambivalence, an uncertainty over whether this was everyone's flag or the enfranchised minority's flag, a flag to be destroyed or a flag to be claimed.

But if the flag did not attract animosity, it was low on ardour too. Scarcely would one see artefacts like key-rings or playing cards in orange, white and blue. Seldom did one see spontaneous celebration of the flag, and when one did, the ambivalence cut in. Were the celebrants celebrating South Africa, or were they celebrating minority rule? The flag was a fact of life, accepted in all quarters but revered in only one corner of South Africa's rich human flower-bed.

Flag-wise, the state of play was in a neutral zone – less than troublesome but far from great.

HE WHO CREATED THUNDER does not fear it.

- African proverb -

MANDELA FOR PRESIDENT
THE PEOPLE'S CHOICE
NEW SOUTH AFRICA

NOTE
100
HOWZIT
BILL!

OFFICIAL SPONSORS - ATLANTA 1996
KFC
Reebok
SOUTH AFRICA

KITES RISE HIGHEST against the wind - not with it.
- Winston Churchill -

RSA 1800
WARRIOR

Lydia Gates

JUST LIVING IS NOT ENOUGH ... one must have sunshine, freedom, and a little flower.

- Hans Christian Anderson -

G A M E

Catherine van Jaarsveld

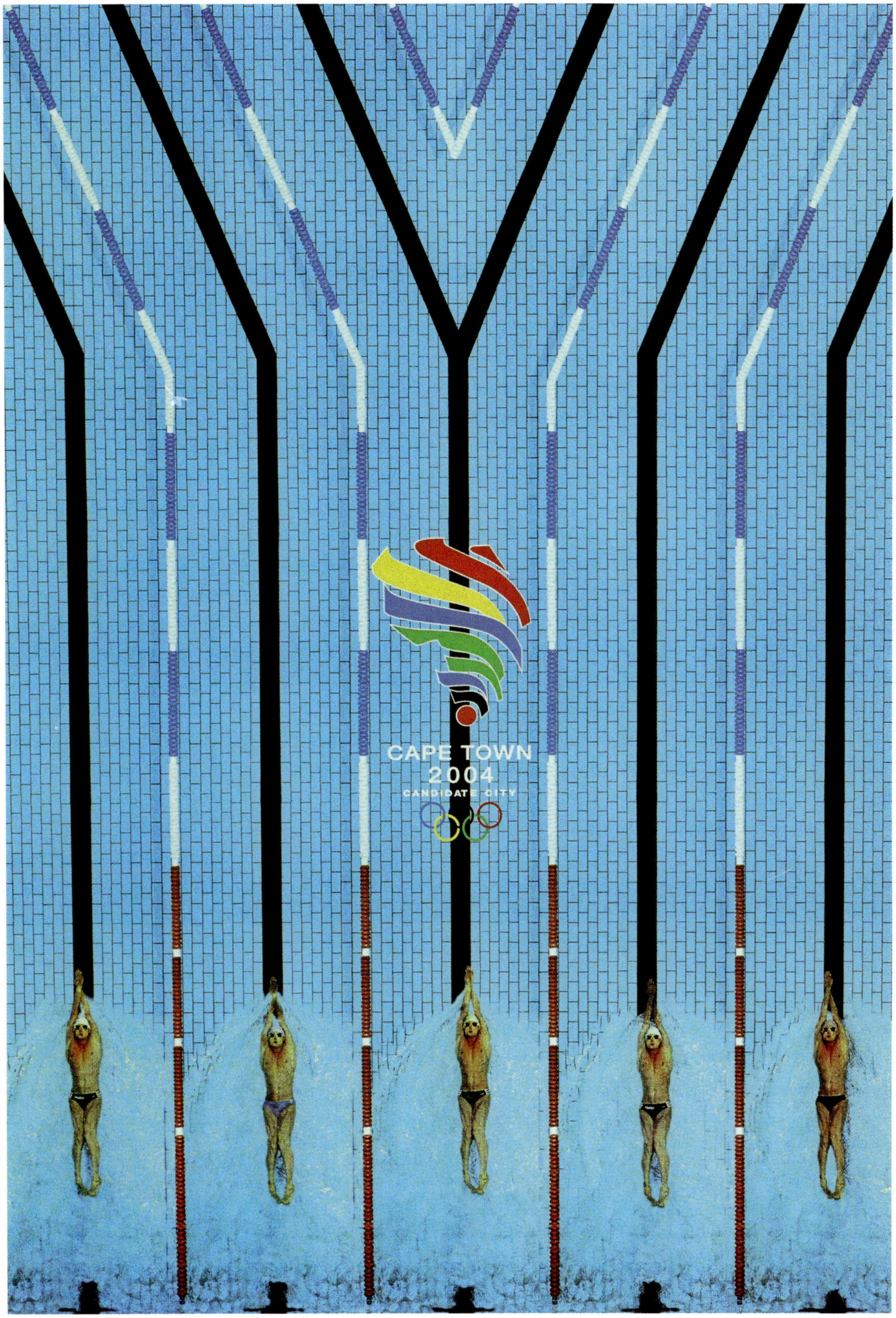
CAPE TOWN
2004
CANDIDATE CITY

FOR THE TIMES, they are a-changin'.
- Bob Dylan -

In February 1990 Fred Brownell, the State Herald of the Republic of South Africa, was busy lending a neighbourly hand to the about-to-be-new nation of Namibia with the design of its national symbols.

THIS WAS SOON AFTER NELSON MANDELA HAD BEEN FREED FROM PRISON AND THE AFRICAN NATIONAL CONGRESS WAS UNBANNED.

Fred detected that a new national identity would soon be coming up for his own country too. He started turning options round in his mind.

For three years he sought a theme for a new South African flag. He selected and de-selected half the colours in the kaleidoscope. He wrestled with one design after another. But he never quite got to the point of crying *Eureka!* Fred was in a different position to the average amateur flag-designer, who would typically think of designing a flag in the same way as you might design a dress or a poster or a packet. He knew the ground-rules.

For instance:

- You must have light colours in between dark ones. Otherwise, when your flag is printed in black-and-white, or viewed from afar, it looks like a blur.
- You must have a design that people can more-or-less draw. They needn't get it exact (or the Union Jack would have been a terrible flop) but if they can't get the essence there's a problem. The more twirls and curves you give them the more trouble you're asking for.

... YOU MUST HAVE A DESIGN THAT PEOPLE CAN MORE-OR-LESS DRAW...

- Getting ambitious, with birds or animals or artworks, is a no-go. Aside from the drawing problem you're inviting cynics (well supplied in any country at any time) to turn your eagle to a crow or your lion to a tortoise. Whatever "political" colours the nation may have, you'd

better be sure to show either none of them or all of them.

- You can't rely on the wind blowing. The fatal temptation of flag design is to focus on the full-out flag. Much of the time it will in fact hang limp from its post. You want it to be recognisable then too.
- Light blue backgrounds get lost against the sky, white backgrounds get scruffy fast, and any hint of subtlety turns to mystery at the top of a flagpole.

Fred also had a solid comparative background, which came in doubly useful in an arena where veering off the straight and narrow meets booby-traps on both sides. For instance, you want the world, including the majority who will only know your flag exists if you win an Olympic medal, to perceive your flag as a flag. You don't want them to mistake it for a supermarket bag or an escapee from a gallery of modern art. But you don't want them, either, to confuse it with anyone else's flag. This is an aim that is often not met. Columbians and Ecuadorians need great eyesight and much practice to tell their flags apart. Were the occasion to arise that Poland, Monaco and Indonesia occupied three adjoining flagposts you'd rub your eyes and wonder if someone slipped something in your coffee.

YOU WANT THE WORLD ...
TO PERCEIVE YOUR FLAG AS A FLAG

So it's handy to know that more than half the world's 193 national flags are in horizontal stripes; that a fifth have vertical stripes, a tenth have crosses, another tenth have a central device like the classic Japanese red disc on a white background, and so on.

Fred also set out to combine the conservative European flag tradition with the bolder and more colourful African approach, and, of course, to convey the right theme. But the theme wouldn't come.

After three years of thinking it over with no answer in sight, Fred was becoming "somewhat despondent". Then he went to Zürich for the 1993 International Congress of Vexillology.

Vexillology is used to being taken, by the few laypersons who meet its name at all, as the study of why people get vexed. It is, in truth, the study of flags (from, yes, Latin – *vexillum* = flag) and as with any academic studies its congresses have their duller moments. On the night of August 25 1993 Fred was hungry, tired, and distracted, and fell to doodling. But what he doodled was not just the normal circles or bricks or spiders hanging from the corner of the page. He doodled an idea, on the back of the congress programme.

The idea was convergence and unification. "You can say now that it is obvious. But for three years it hadn't been obvious." Fair enough. The wheel, too, doubtless became obvious the moment that somebody had invented it. The more Fred looked at his representation of convergence and unification, the more he thought "that's it". He started experimenting with colours, adjusting dimensions, exploring variations, and generally refining the convergence theme. On September 7 that same year the Negotiating Council at the World Trade Centre in Kempton Park appointed a National Symbols Commission to invite public flag submissions, choose a short-list, and present a report. The Commission's short life was not a happy one. The "Old" and "New" members experienced little of the inter-personal thawing which was wreaking miracles in other areas of the negotiating process. The time-frame was outlandish – public entries closed on October 13 and the Commission was to report on the 19th. For Fred Brownell

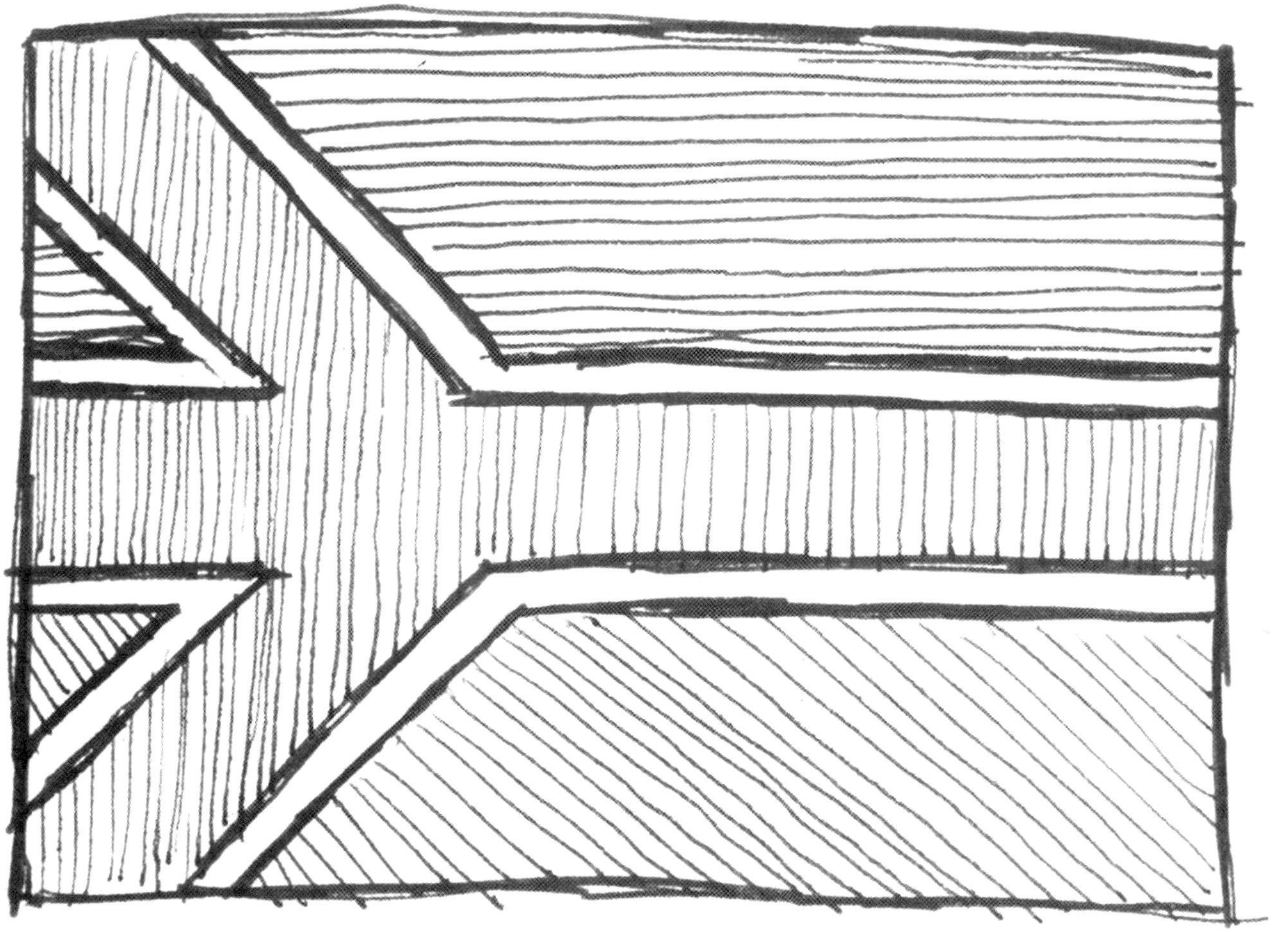

ONE PERCENT INSPIRATION, NINETY-NINE PERCENT PERSPIRATION

The earliest thoughts were sketched by Fred Brownell on the back of a programme during a flag conference held in 1993.

ENTHUSIASTIC PARTICIPATION *The call for public participation in the design of a new national flag was met with enthusiasm: over 7 000 entries were received for consideration by the National Symbols Commission.*

there was an extra problem. He was appointed to the Commission. Being part of the jury he could not also be a contestant. He did not submit his idea, but in his private time he did keep refining it.

On October 14 the Commission met. It had received some 7 000 flag designs, which if pasted on walls at 50 cm intervals would mean 3,5 kilometres of walking. The Commission had from 11 am to 4 pm to decide on six designs for submission to the Negotiating Council. Precisely how such disdain came to be visited on the 7 000 contributors is a matter of dispute. What is beyond dispute is that a thorough assessment was out of the question: the Commission selected its short-list and within days presented these to the Negotiating Council and, almost simultaneously, to the media.

Response was immediate and unhesitating, from both the Council and the public. A mass "no thanks" reverberated throughout the World Trade Centre, where the negotiations were being held. The same sentiment, with a high quotient of caustic epithets, echoed from Beit Bridge to Cape Point.

EVOLUTION IN PROGRESS *The Zürich design was tweaked and changed until everyone was either satisfied or too tired to argue any more.*

The Commission, having fulfilled its mandate, retired hurt. The Negotiating Council swapped to the opposite tack. The public hadn't delivered, what about the professionals? A selection of graphic design studios were asked to try their hands at flag design, in a hurry. History repeated itself. The negotiators said "No", politely. The public said "No", less politely.

Time was pushing. The Negotiating Council had other concerns. At the end of 1993 the Constitution of democratic South Africa appeared. What appeared where the design of the flag was supposed to be described was, instead, a naked cop-out: "The national flag of the Republic shall be the flag the design of which is determined by the President by proclamation in the Gazette."

Meanwhile, Fred Brownell was still tinkering with his idea, which had moved steadily onward from the original Zürich doodle. Colours changed, for instance. At one stage there was green at the top and blue below, with red in the middle. Fred imagined critics placing sarcastic constructions on the red paths converging. He upgraded the green to central status. And the red...? This was a thorny one. Red, a strong and striking primary colour, was here in a shape hitherto unknown. There was something very right about that. But red was also full of problematic meanings. Red meant blood, for one thing. To interpret it as blood that has been spilt – the price of the convergence – could be poignant and moving. But one didn't want to open the way to cynicism about blood-letting to come. Moreover, red was communism's colour. Whatever ultimate judgement posterity might pass on communism, it was a philosophy associated with unusually strong feelings for and against. Fred had his brightest vexillological inspiration so far: turn the red to chilli red, the half-orange red, and score two in one.

Let those who choose see Marx's red. Let those who choose see 342 years of symbolic orange continuity. Fred also brought in yellow. Yellow was commonly perceived as representing gold, or the nation's mineral wealth, and green and gold were (obligingly) both South Africa's sporting colours and two of the main colours of the liberation movements.

Along the way he did that sensible thing we all do when we have a bright idea. He checked it out with his family, and made further changes – when, for example, his youngest daughter pointed out that one version of the design, turned on its side, looked like the "ban the bomb" sign. Fred adjusted it to a Y.

ALONG THE WAY HE DID THAT SENSIBLE THING ... HE CHECKED IT OUT WITH HIS FAMILY.

In February 1994 the negotiators, now statutorily the Transitional Executive Council (TEC) returned to the flag. By now they knew when the flag was going to fly – April 27. But they didn't know what flag would fly. There wasn't as much as a hint or a clue or an agreed avenue to further pursue. A technical committee was appointed with Fred Brownell as convenor. It had a simple brief: find a flag, within a week. The committee met in Cape Town on February 28 1994. The feeling was that unity, interlinking or convergence should be the theme. Input came from several quarters and within two days four designs had been prepared – two of these based on the Zürich theme.

At this very delicate stage in the whole transitional process the designs were presented to the negotiating parties for behind-the-scenes consideration. To have any chance at all, at least one of them needed to enjoy tacit support before formal submission to the TEC for its verdict. Fred had two white lines. They were there as a design feature, to separate dark from dark, but some people would see white as representing white people. If so, there had to be black too. Thus did what had so far been a yellow triangle become a yellow collar on a black triangle, and this is the flag that, after consultation, was to be laid before a TEC meeting on March 15.

By March of 1994 the TEC's members were heartily sick of all-day political horse-trading. They were weary, and agreeing on issues that a few months earlier would have caused major rows. But they were also flag-wary, after two false starts. It was almost as if they were waiting for a Vision from Above, something that was at first sight so blindingly perfect that they would be relieved of all doubt.

Was Fred's design that thing? We will never know. People are not computers, impervious to chance. We are susceptible to happenstance. That is our strength. All we can know is what did happen. The TEC meeting was to be held in Pretoria, supposedly at 2.00 pm. Fred arrived early and gave the flag, a full-size version, to Roelf Meyer, the government's chief negotiator. Roelf said he would take it to his ANC counterpart, Cyril Ramaphosa, and asked Fred to wait around in case there were any questions.

This was a closed meeting; no press. It was also a delayed meeting, finally by four hours. When the discussion on the flag was finally due to start, there was an unused chair in front of one delegation. Fred took the chair, overheard the members of the delegation talking, and realised that these were hereditary chiefs from the QwaQwa homeland – one of the less vociferous of the many components of the TEC, and one of the more neutral, especially since

they only had observer status.

Fred, a Free State farmer's son from way back, greeted in seSotho. The chiefs were as surprised as is customary to find a pale person speaking seSotho. Hands were shaken and discussion occurred. The chiefs were intrigued to hear about the flag, and wanted a sneak preview. Fred had a small paper version still with him, and surreptitiously displayed it. The chiefs asked about colours, meanings, patterns, and as talk went on they warmed – perhaps to what they were seeing, perhaps to a friendly white homeboy who spoke seSotho. Then order was called and the session began.

...THERE WAS AN AGONISING SILENCE AS THE TEC PEERED AT THE MULTI-COLOURED CLOTH, CAUTIOUSLY, UNCERTAINLY...

Roelf and Cyril took the floor and showed the flag. There was an agonising silence as the TEC peered at the multi-coloured cloth, cautiously, uncertainly. Fred had a sinking feeling: were they going to veto this one too?

Just in the nick of time, enthusiastic clapping broke out. It broke out in one particular corner, the one occupied by the QwaQwa chiefs. It spread, and soon the clapping grew to a crescendo. The flag was in business: the TEC, whether displaying great efficiency or great exhaustion, had accepted it there and then. Then it was off to the assembled pressroom. As Cyril and Roelf positioned themselves to present the flag to the world, Roelf remarked that he and Cyril were holding the wrong sides. Cyril looked. Indeed, he was holding the stripes; Roelf had the black triangle. They changed places, and the cameras whirred. Thereby was expressed a slim but penetrating slice of symbolism.

Was this new society to mean all South Africans as equal citizens regardless of race? Or was it really a merging of nationalisms, and perhaps, like so many mergers, a takeover in disguise? For the first but not the last time it appeared that there were fundamentally different ways of seeing the flag. For some, it was joyous, lively, exuberant, a riot of colour on which everyone had an identical claim. For others it was the green, yellow and black of the ANC overlaying the chilli-red, white and blue associated with the past.

Having instantly adopted the flag, the TEC inexplicably took four of the six remaining weeks before the election to ask the State President to officially legalise it, causing cardiac arrest among the nation's flag-makers. Meantime, the Bureau of Heraldry was flooded with queries about design, colour codes and symbolism.

To those who asked Fred stood firm, explaining that the only intentional symbolism was convergence and unification, represented by the V starting at the left, coming together in the centre, and proceeding as a horizontal band to the end. For the rest, the colours were just colours, recognising both the flags which had flown in the past and the realities of the present. Still, as he concedes, there is no copyright on the way people perceive their flag. The public was entitled to attach, as it did, whatever meaning it liked to the colours, and to maintain, as it still often does, that the blue ought to be on top "for the sky".

"What mattered," he says, "was that the flag would find its way into the hearts and minds of the population at large, and became a unifying symbol."

Which is what the distracted sketch made on the back of a programme at a congress in Zürich has indeed done.

SYMBOLS OF A NEW DEMOCRACY *The Transitional Executive Council called for public participation in designing a flag for "The New South Africa."*

DESPERATION STAKES *With no joy from the public process, the country's design studios were asked to do their best.*

LABONG

ONLY THOSE WHO WERE STEEPED IN THE PAST
would have any understanding of the greatness of the present.
- Alan Paton -

SELECTING A NEW SOUTH AFRICAN NATIONAL FLAG WAS PART OF THE NEGOTIATION PROCESS TOWARDS A NEW DISPENSATION SET IN MOTION WHEN NELSON MANDELA WAS RELEASED FROM PRISON IN 1990 AFTER 27 YEARS IN CONFINEMENT.

In attempting to find a design that was nationally representative, a nationwide competition was launched in 1993. More than 7000 designs were received. Based on the submissions, six designs were drawn up by the National Symbols Commission and presented to the public and the Negotiating Council – but none of them elicited enthusiastic support. As a result, a number of design studios were contracted to submit further proposals – again without a suitable result. Parliament went into recess at the end of 1993 without a suitable candidate for a new national flag.

In mid-February 1994, Messrs Cyril Ramaphosa and Roelf Meyer, chief negotiators for the African National Congress and the National Party government of the day respectively, were tasked with resolving the flag issue. A final design was adopted on March 15 1994, derived from a concept developed by the State Herald, Mr Fred Brownell.

The proclamation of the new national flag was only published on the 20th of April 1994 – seven days before the new national flag was to be inaugurated at all flag stations across the nation. This created an enormous problem for flag manufacturers. That the task was accomplished, is a matter of record.

By means of the April 20 proclamation, the six-coloured South African national flag was effectively adopted as an "interim" national flag under the interim South African Constitution, Act 200 of 1993.

The new flag was officially described and illustrated in Schedule 1 to the Constitution of the Republic of South Africa, Act 108 of 1996, at which time it's interim status quietly slipped into oblivion. By this time the question over whether or not it's status should be affirmed did not need airing: it had become an integral part of the fabric of the New South African society, the Rainbow Nation.

Despite conjecture to the contrary, there is no symbolic meaning to the colours in the flag; the designer's own interpretation is that it conveys a sense of convergence of diverse elements in South African society which then take the road ahead in unison.

CAPE TOWN
2004

SOUTH AFRICA
CANARY

LAUGHTER IS the closest distance between two people.

- Victor Borge -

When the biggest order in history came rushing towards South Africa's flag-makers they did not respond with a whoop of glee.

FOR ONE THING, THE RUSH WAS RIDICULOUSLY LATE. YOU DON'T JUST PRINT A FLAG LIKE YOU PRINT A NEWSPAPER, THOUSANDS OF COMPLETED COPIES HURTLING OFF THE PRESS EVERY HOUR.

For the printing alone you need (at the time – the technology has since moved on) several sequential operations, each with teams of people laying strips of textile one by one on a flatbed. Then you have a drying process, a de-starching process (so the flag will flap freely), a colour-fastening process, an auto-stitching process plus a hand-stitching process, and an intricate little corner-fastening process so the flag does not unravel the first time the wind blows. Above all, you need time.

...THE FIRST SIGHT OF THE FLAG WAS SIX WEEKS BEFORE IT WAS DUE TO FLY ACROSS THE NATION...

But time there was not. The first sight of the flag was six weeks before it was due to fly across the nation. And for five of those six weeks the final design remained uncertain. The TEC had said, yes, here is the flag. But saying was not enough: until the flag was signed into law, in the Government Gazette, producing any at all constituted a significant risk.

What if you embraced the proposed flag, charged full tilt into production, and then some technical hitch showed up in the design? Imagine making flags by the shedload, and there they are, loaded in the sheds, when the Gazette appears and tells you that the black has swopped with the gold, or that the white is a centimetre thicker, or that the chilli-red has adjusted to crimson. Your ordinary, decent flag-maker would become the proud owner of mountains of useless cloth, on the run from creditors' heavies with knuckledusters.

The Government Gazette remained stubbornly silent. The TEC however, backed by the public purse, took on part of the risk; it put out a tender for 6 000 flags as per the March 15 design. Six thousand? Suppliers argued that this was not nearly enough. "It's not just polling stations; look at courts, post offices, army bases, police stations... You're

going to have the new flag out on April 27 and all these places flying the old one the very next day! You're asking for strife!" The reply was "We are the customer, you mind the production."

The 6 000 were allocated, 2 000 each, to three companies at R90 per flag. Which was also a problem. At R90 there was not a lot of incentive, whereas once the legalities were finalised the private sector – casinos, supermarkets, sports stadiums and so on – would pay R120, easy. Two of the three tenders were submitted by the local big-boys, National Flag and Flagcraft, both of which were headed by dedicated flag-fans.

IN ANY CASE, THERE JUST WASN'T ENOUGH FLAG MATERIAL TO BE HAD.

Flags had indeed been the making of Mike Clingman's life. Mike started National Flag in 1981, for the very simple reason that he had a yen to erect his own national flag on a flagpole in his garden, and couldn't find one. At the time he was a paint-shop foreman. Since he left school in Standard 8, he had changed jobs on average twice a year. After his accidental discovery of flags Mike settled down, became a flag expert, and established National Flag as a highly successful flag-making company.

Tony Hampson-Tindale at Flagcraft had a fascination with flags even as a kid in New Zealand. He moved to South Africa in the course of his first career as a merchant banker. When, by a series of chances, the opportunity came up of buying a small flag factory he jumped at it – and soon turned it into a big flag factory.

In late March 1994 both Mike and Tony doubted that the flag demand would be adequately met by April 27. It just so happened that National Flag was moving premises in April, which didn't help matters. In any case, there just wasn't enough flag material to be had. And even working all night and all weekend, there were only so many hands available in the factories to produce the flags.

The third successful tender came from deep on the blind side.

Karel Kuiper is a Holland-born chemical engineer. After running his own small business in Pretoria for decades, in 1993 he sold it, went into semi-retirement, and underwent a fit of new-South-Africa nervousness. This fit took him on a trip back to Holland to explore prospects there. "There I met an old school friend who said 'No problem, come and join me, I make flags'. I said 'You're crazy, what do I know about flags?' Anyway after looking around Holland I decided I belong here in South Africa after all. I came back."

On March 7 1994 Karel's friend dropped him a line. "He said 'Do you realise that in a hundred years not a single country has totally changed its flag? There's big business coming up.' He suggested that I get into it. He had the capacity, I could send him the work, we'd do fine."

Although Karel's friend's history is not in the A Division – countries had indeed changed their flags before – his persuasive powers were strong. Karel climbed on board. At first, it looked good. The day after the 2 000 were ordered, a Colonel Swanepoel from the police phoned. He'd heard Karel was making flags, and he needed 1 000 for April 27. Karel phoned Holland, Holland said fine. Karel phoned the Colonel, Karel said fine. The next day another division phoned with another order. Same process. Then Justice, then Correctional Services...

Soon Karel is sitting with orders for nearly 30 000 flags. He is horribly aware that only 2 000 of these – the TEC's – are fully secured against the Government Gazette changing the pattern. Meantime, his partners in Holland have discovered that they are overstretched. They can print the newer orders but they cannot sew them; they're sending the printed cloth over in massive reels.

Karel hunts down every suitable sewing shop he can find, first in Pretoria, then across the province, then across the

country. They range from a factory in Durban – 500 a day, once all other production is halted for the flag – to sewing clubs, bucket shops, little one-woman operations in back streets and townships... In total he has over two hundred machines sewing flags.

... TO SEWING CLUBS, BUCKET SHOPS, LITTLE ONE-WOMAN OPERATIONS IN BACKSTREETS AND TOWNSHIPS ...

He's turning out a thousand a day, but the orders keep coming in. The Holland partners frantically start farming out extra sewing too, first in Holland, then in France, then across half of Europe.

Through the State President's office Karel fights for, and gets, special permission from the SA Bureau of Standards to pass up the triangular corners. That accelerates things. By April 20, the day the Gazette (thankfully) publishes the unchanged specifications, Karel's network is churning out nearly 5 000 flags a day. But the orders are now up to 65 000, there are more than 30 000 still to go, and in six days time there'll be more than 30 000 expectant flagpoles awaiting them.

Karel is on the edge. He's been working eighteen or more hours a day for a month. He's fought with his wife, his partner, his suppliers and his customers. Then... would you believe, he can't believe... then Europe runs out of polyester cloth. The length and breadth of Europe, there's no flag material to be had. Karel invokes the State President's office once more.

Two things happen. One is that the Bureau of Standards, with the State President's office on the phone, changes the specification to allow a different material. That takes

two days, which is jet-rocket league next to the normal process but is still two days out of Karel's beleaguered life. The other is that, by remote control, material is flown from Japan, printed in Holland – and by this stage Belgium and Germany too – and jetted to Jan Smuts (now Johannesburg International) airport where trucks stand by to distribute it to everywhere from factories in Milnerton to sewing clubs in Wonderboom and Mamelodi.

Saturday at 11am Karel's second-last huge consignment comes in. The sewing people are waiting, some sitting at their tables, on overtime, with no material. The expectant trucks are at Freight Delivery – but Customs is closed. Karel phones his Customs contact, who is on his way to golf with three people waiting for him. Karel screams at him. "I wasn't nice, I must admit. I told him to go and get *dingused* and slammed the phone down. Then I felt terrible, and Customs was still closed. I went back to the State President's office. They were getting sick of me too – but they got Customs opened."

Meantime, cash-flow is dodgy. Not least, the rand is plunging like a stone (well, a 1994 brand of stone, almost buoyant compared to what was to follow) and most of

STOP

Karel's outlay is in guilders. With little more than 100 hours to E-Day, 6 000 flags are impounded in France: payment is due. Karel's cardiograph must by now look like an earthquake. He has two hours to get these flags on a plane; there are four sewing factories waiting. It's back to the State President's office once more, which again turns up trumps.

At eight on the morning of April 26 – just 16 hours to the ceremonial midnight hoisting, and less than 24 until the flag is to be raised on tens of thousands of poles across the land – Karel feels like a dishcloth on a nail. At least, he thinks, the pain is past its peak, and dwindling. He's wrong. From the crack of dawn his premises are awash with agitated officials from Departments, Sections and Units, clamouring for their allocation of flags. Karel buys time; he's waiting for consignments from three of his Pretoria sub-contractors. When the phone rings with a message from one of them, he grabs it with glee. His ears hear the message, but his tired mind can't take it in. He says "What did you say?" three times before it penetrates.

The suppliers have mutinied. They haven't been paid what he agrees he owes, and they're demanding (in his interpretation) an extortionate increase too. They threaten: no pay, no flags. Worse still: no pay, and they'll call the SABC and burn the flags before the cameras. An urgent application follows. Karel stuffs R65 000 in cash into a bag. At court, there are reporters everywhere. He pulls his jacket over his head, grabs his bag, and pushes in. He comes away with a woman sheriff, three large male deputies, and an interdict for the delivery of the flags. Delivery does not proceed altogether smoothly though, the R65 000 being considered inadequate by the suppliers. Resistance is presented. At one of the premises "a woman threw a *blompot* at me from the top of the stairs, but missed. The sheriff wanted to arrest her. I said 'we've got the flags, leave it.'" The day ends at 3.00 am with Karel driving his Mercedes, packed with so many flags that he can't use the handbrake, through a crowd of protesters toyi-toying in demand for flags, into the basement below the State President's office.

...THE FLAG WAS ALL OVER THE PLACE. I FELT A PRIDE.

Next morning... "I still had angry customers, but at least the flag was all over the place. I felt a pride. I might not have got everything right, but I got something right."

Lucky 7

WHEN DISPLAYED HORIZONTALLY, THE RED BAND MUST BE UPPERMOST. FLYING A FLAG UPSIDE DOWN IS AN INTERNATIONAL MARITIME SIGNAL OF DISTRESS.

When draped vertically, a flag should not merely be rotated through 90 degrees, but also reversed. In the case of the South African flag, the black triangle must be uppermost and the red band to the observer's left. One "reads" a flag like the pages of a book – from top to bottom and from left to right, and after rotation the results should be the same. Innumerable items and icons, including early versions of the Welcome Man, have mistakenly used a vertical representation of the flag with the red to the observer's right.

There are special sizes of the flag for different occasions – including a small storm flag for use during high winds.

The 27th of April, now known as Freedom Day, is designated as an official ceremonial day in South Africa, and on this day a special ceremonial-sized flag is flown at all official flag stations.

Use of the flag in artefacts and products is subject to the approval of The Presidency and, in the case of manufactured items, the Department of Trade and Industry. Under no circumstances may printed representations of the flag bear writing or printing of any kind; in all cases, writing should appear adjacent to, or underneath, the image of the flag.

There are gazetted instructions for flying the national flag, but Parliament may adopt its own rules. Any enquiries relating to the use of the national flag should be addressed to The Presidency.

Central Hotel

mita
AFR
4

SOUTH
PEACE

BAFANA BAFANA

HILWAN'S
COACH
HIRE
GHANA

vodacom
south africa 2006 SAFA
EXIT EXIT
EXIT EXIT

We welcome the opening of new horizons
Approved by the Office of the President of the Republic of South Africa
Change has opened new horizons for us all, revealing a brighter future. A future we can manage better, together.
HELPING YOU MANAGE YOUR FUTURE BETTER
SOUTHERN
Together, we can do more

THE BEST DRESSED SPRINGBOK SUPPORTER WINS WITH VODACOM.

If you're the best dressed South African supporter at any one of the Vodacom International Rugby games, you will win an all expenses paid trip for two to a local Vodacom Tri-Nations game.

EVERBEST.R.S.A

EACH AND EVERY NATION has the right to change its own destiny.

- Mangosuthu Buthelezi -

CORPCOM

SOUTH AFRICAN
ZS-SHC

SOUTH AFRICAN AIRWAYS

786 2136
Rikki's
COASTAL SAFARIS
6
CA 264-122

C-class

Berlin in the summer of 1989 was a time-warp. To the west of the Wall, the boisterous opulence of consumerism was writ large.

TO THE EAST, PEOPLE WORE DARK 1950'S CLOTHES AND DROVE SMOKY TOYLAND CARS. ON THE WEST SIDE YOU COULD BUY EVERY KIND OF LITERATURE MANKIND HAS DREAMED UP.

At the checkpoints, grim East German guards in high-peaked caps confiscated every printed word, from the Bible to Playboy to a bus timetable.

Not everything in East Berlin lived up to the caricatures of drabness and dictatorship though. There was also a simplicity and gentleness in person-to-person life. While there was no opulence, there was also no destitution. Ossies – easterners – talked of the up sides of egalitarianism and worried about what they stood to lose when they were taken over by the money-making bustle across the Wall. One came to see valuable features as well as odious features in their system, and to wonder if its impending collapse was such a big step forward after all. Finally, the odious features prevailed on the sensibilities. One convincing aspect was the flag.

East Germans flew the flag from their apartment windows, a phenomenon which at first seemed attractive and interestingly patriotic. But when people spoke of why they flew the flag, it became ugly: they flew it through fear – fear of the Stasi, the secret police who, if they failed to fly it, would come to visit. Far from being a symbol of affection, the flag was a symbol of tyranny. While asphyxiation in two-horsepower dodgem-cars may be a price worth paying for a society free of destitution, no economic equation justified the price of high-peaked caps busting down the door to find out why your flag was missing.

FAR FROM BEING A SYMBOL OF AFFECTION, THE FLAG WAS A SYMBOL OF TYRANNY.

The experience also suggested that the way in which a nation uses its flag is a barometer of its health. If the East German way was one end of the spectrum, what is the other? That's not hard to find: anyone who has visited America can only be astonished by their use of the flag. There the Stars and Stripes is everywhere, not by

compulsion but in rampant, free-wheeling exuberance. It's on garments and bumpers and bandages and windscreens and anything that carries a surface. You fly it when and where you want to, and if you don't want, that's fine too. Technically, much of this enthusiasm was at one time illegal. Forty-eight of the fifty states had laws that prohibited desecrating the flag or treating it with contempt. Most states added details of flag etiquette, often far more intricate than any ordinary citizen would ever know, such as that a flag draped across an east-west street must have the "union" (the top-corner bit with the stars) to the north, and on a north-south street the "union" must be to the east. About 35 states went even further, spelling out specific prohibitions such as that the flag may not be embroidered on a cushion, may not be used as a receptacle, may not be printed on a discardable box, may not be superimposed with words, or may not be used as a costume.

Until the 1960s these laws were more or less upheld, with occasional blips of controversy such as when someone iced a cake with the flag in contravention of a law that the flag may lie flat only on a coffin. Then the laws came to be honoured more in the breach – and increasingly the flagrant breach – than in the observation, a development which elicited diverse views. One view said: uh oh, decline and fall, the law is being flouted. The other was: ah, how advanced; no laws are needed to enforce respect when citizens go beyond respect of their own accord, and into love. Tacitly, the latter view won the day.

But not everyone loved the flag. It was easy to turn a blind eye to the flag's fans. But what of the flag-haters? Generally nations have viewed an assault on the flag as an assault on the State and therefore punishable, often severely. Not until the 1970s, and then not everywhere, did the thought arise that here was a paradox. To say "this flag represents your freedom, so you have to respect it" may not be entirely logical. What of the alternative possibility: "this flag represents your freedom, which includes your freedom to disrespect it if you so choose?"

In 1974 a young American was convicted of sewing a flag to the seat of his trousers. The case made its way up the legal pyramid to the highest court in the land, which... ducked it. The court overturned the conviction, but on a mere technicality. It said that "contemptuous treatment" could not be banned; "contempt" had first to be "defined with substantial specificity". This ruling recognised changing times, but not very decisively. It dislodged the old certainty, but in favour only of uncertainty.

... IT WAS OKAY TO DO ANYTHING WHATSOEVER TO THE FLAG, INCLUDING BURN IT.

In 1989 the Supreme Court revisited the subject. This time it did not duck the issue: instead, it made as far-reaching a ruling as was possible, invalidating some sixty laws or parts of laws, state and federal. Reinterpreting the constitution's emphasis on freedom, it said that henceforth it was okay to do anything whatsoever to the flag, including burn it.

Outrage ensued, with ridicule along the lines of "why not legalise murder, why not legalise rape?" And yet... if Berlin was one extreme – using force to compel a facade of imaginary respect – then this was the opposite: simply laugh off all disrespect. Perhaps it was a stroke of genius. It cut out what could have been decades of wrangling over what was contemptuous and what was not. Making the flag into a flowerpot? An ashtray? A toilet bowl...? More than that, contempt's teeth were drawn. However furious you

FREE
SHEIGK
YASIEN
LONG

may be at the flag and all that it stands for, it's hard to put your heart and soul into trampling it if the police are standing by to protect your constitutional right to trample. And more than that, it was a proof of health. If everyone is free to burn the flag, and once every five years someone exercises that right while each week a hundred million people fly the flag, that proves two profound things. It proves that freedom is fundamental, and that dissent is limited. No amount of protective legislation can have the same effect.

BY MAY THE FLAG WAS RAISING LUMPS IN THE THROAT.

Measured by the flag barometer, in 1989 several countries looked good. Several African countries were among them, where women commonly wore the flag as a wrap-around. How heartening to have a firm, intact, shared identity under which to work out issues. But how sorrowfully distant that status seemed to a South African.

Then came '94, the new flag, and a dictionary of disapproval. In the weeks after its appearance the flag was denounced as meaningless, undignified and undemocratic; as a beach-towel, a jockstrap, a technicolour wineglass, a schoolboy's cattie, a carpet design, a crayon game and more.

The Cape Times was glad it was merely transitional, and debunked the hope that it might "grow in the minds of South Africans". The Sowetan concluded mournfully that "we might get used to it". The Argus reported a "disgusted" response. Johan van Wyk in Beeld termed it the "*kniekombersie*", lap rug. Barry Ronge in the Sunday Times chose "a v-front flag, with more mismatched colours than you'll find in a hooker's make-up kit" and could not "imagine our athletes pitching up at the next Olympics waving this thing on high".

That was March 1994. By May the flag was raising lumps in the throat. We were proud, we were tall, we could do anything, we and our flag, which symbolised our prowess. By July the flag was more than a mere symbol. It was a possession. It was keyrings and, yes, beach-towels. It was headbands and, yes, underpants. It was on bumpers, on hubcaps, on windscreens. It was coffee-mugs and garden walls. It was painted on faces and plastered on lampposts. Within months, South Africa had not merely caught up to the American high-water-mark of flag exuberance but had, in many ways, overtaken it.

America's exuberance may be tempered by a worry in some quarters that their flag-waving is hubristic – over-cocky – telling the rest of the world "Stand aside, squirts, we're the biggest and the richest." In South Africa we knew we weren't the biggest, we knew we weren't the richest, we were arrogant to no-one. We were celebrating that we were a nation at last, after all those years of untenable compartments. Even more, we were celebrating that we were a nation at peace, a nation we were happy to share. More innocuous, you could not get.

No wonder we carried the flag on our playing-cards, on our mouse-pads, on our socks and our shorts and our jerseys and our jackets and our ballpoint pens and our bubble-gum. We had a lot of accumulated tension to work off, both the people who had been saying "excuse us, can we too have a place in the sun" and the people who had been saying "no, you are too numerous and you'll shut out our light."

Relief was a two-way street, but an awkward one to raise in words. So it was raised in six-coloured hairbrushes and

SOUTH AFRICA

Elastoplast
Rainbow Strips

SPORT

GSM

60 PIECES

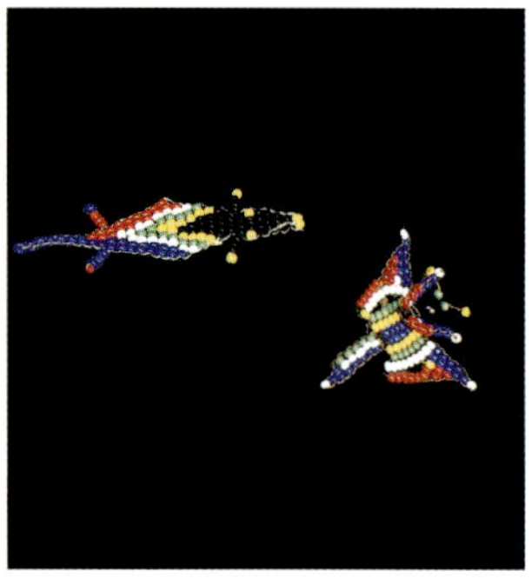

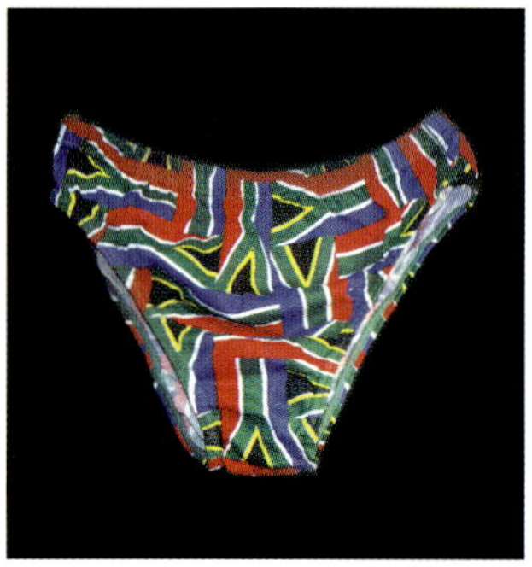

takkies and toothpaste tubes and cellphone pouches and CD covers and condoms. Which made us criminals, technically. Under the Heraldry Act every child frolicking at a fete in a flag-painted face – unless with written approval from The Presidency – is liable to a fine of R1 000. Under the Merchandise Marks Act everyone who sells an unapproved flag key-ring is open to a fine of R100 (the approximate price of two cows when the Act was passed in 1941) and, more deterring, the confiscation of the goods.

In practice, society simply passed beyond the law. The flag, we know in our hearts, belongs in more ways than one to all of us.

But, of course, some do not want to own it. From time to time during the late 1990s a flap and flurry arose when the old flag showed up, mainly at rugby matches. There were moves to ban it, and demands for punishment. The terrific maturity that the new flag had ushered in seemed in jeopardy. Were we going to blow it, with laws and charge-sheets and banning orders that would turn the old flag into a symbol of martyrdom?

No, we were not. The flaps and the flurries subsided. Sightings became rarer. In 2001 the only echo of public controversy came when an ex-South African at a cricket match in New Zealand presented an old flag to the Proteas for their autographs. They simply declined. We had arrived at the perfect conclusion: without recourse to compulsion, South Africa's six-coloured flag had been unequivocally adopted as the flag of the entire nation.

What would happen if a flag-burning fad became a token of dissent? We don't know. We have not met that test. What we do know is that so far we have passed every flag-related test with, literally, flying colours. It has carried us from a time of barriers and keep-out to the start of a time of widening and meeting.

...SO FAR WE HAVE PASSED EVERY FLAG-RELATED TEST WITH, LITERALLY, FLYING COLOURS.

We know the course is not concluded. We know there are tests to come, tests of patience, tests of our capacity to see the human being beyond categories and collectivities, tests of foresight. We know there are errors to be corrected, painful errors old, new and ahead. The challenges give us meaning and purpose, but they daunt us too and at times we look for solace.

We never need look far. The sight of the flag is always a reminder of how much better off we are than if we were still wrangling over who belonged. But there are times that the flag packs special punch, like when – perhaps jogging in a flag tracksuit, perhaps wearing a six-colour hat at a foreign airport – we see someone in the same colours. We wave, we smile, and we know we are wide and large and whole, we are brothers, we are sisters.

Mirage III BZ
817

THE CIRCLE OF SUNSHINE

Ekurhuleni
METROPOLITAN MUNICIPALITY

First African in Space

DAY
PRESIDENT
R.N
MANDELA
76 YEARS

ICG
159
SAM

De Beers
A DIAMOND IS FOREVER

CASTLE
LAGER
A Bok supporter to the last drop
NOT FOR SALE TO PERSONS UNDER THE AGE OF 18.

HUMANITY HAS ADVANCED, when it has advanced, not because it has been sober, responsible and cautious, but because it has been playful, rebellious and immature.

- *Tom Robbins* -

WHATEVER YOU DO WILL BE INSIGNIFICANT

but it is very important that you do it.

- Mahatma Ghandi -

SEARCH IN YOUR PAST for what is good and beautiful. Build your future from there.

- Paul Kruger -

Amber Dunton

ART COMPETITION WINNERS

FIRST PLACE: GRADE 1-4

Mary Hoffe

St Mary's School

FIRST PLACE: GRADE 5-7

Pearl Mufandu

Glenhazel Primary School

FIRST PLACE: GRADE 8-10

Arline Daffue

Marais Viljoen High School

FIRST PLACE: GRADE 11-12

Marianne Ball

St Andrews School

WILDNET AFRICA ASKED THE CHILDREN OF SOUTH AFRICA to use their flag to depict the balance between mankind and nature. Here are the winners and some other fine submissions. There is also a selection in the main body of *Flying with Pride*, and a more comprehensive collection at **www.FlyingWithPride.co.za**.

ART COMPETITION SUBMISSIONS

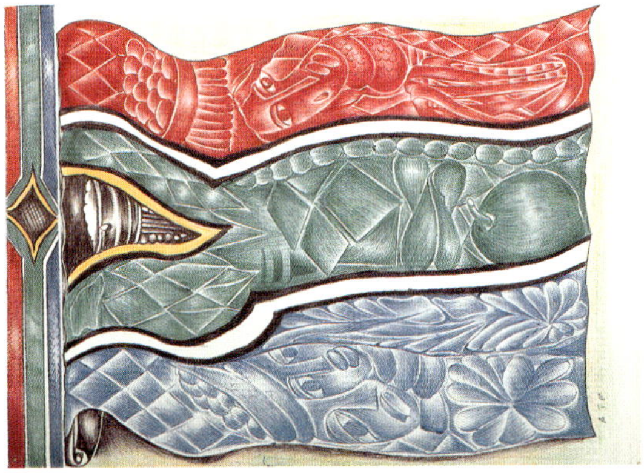

CLOCKWISE FROM TOP LEFT: Jodi Bell; Caroline Coetzee; Juliane Dömötör; Anika Pretorius; Joslin Andrews; Jabu Mokoena

CLOCKWISE FROM TOP LEFT: Devan Kassel; Doreen Kekana; Sumari de Wet; Alexandra Bühler; Alinde Lombaard; Tessa Strydom

MORE THAN ANY OTHER FLAG

Africa Venue Directory

South African Broadcasting Corporation

De Beers

National ParaOlympics of South Africa

Bed And Breakfast Association South Africa

Trade & Investment South Africa

Gauteng Tourism

Surfari

First Cargo

Convention on International Trade in Endangered Species - South Africa

Government Digest

South African Golf Development Board

Intensive Air

Western Cape Tourism Board

LinuxHelp

Motorsport South Africa

Miss South Africa

South African Tourism

South African Federated Chamber of Commerce

City of Johannesburg

N3 Toll Concession

National Accommodation Association

First African in Space

National Scouts Association

Umsebenzi

Haggle

MUCH, MUCH MORE!

Africa Aerospace and Defence

SA Welcome Man

Ekurhuleni
Metropolitan Municipality

Mercedes-Benz South African
Open Championship 2001

National Olympic Committee
of South Africa

South African Weather Service

National Department of Agriculture
(discontinued)

Proudly South African

Thorough Tech

De Beers Shining Light

Bulwark Parking

Nedlac

Vhutsila
National Skills Development Strategy

ZULUCOM

Palesa dolls

South African
Water Ski Federation

The Circle of Sunshine

ViewFinder Balloon Team

Tourism Grading Council

Expos Online

TarHeel South Africans Club

South African Grainfed Beef

South Africa Online

DRAWING INSTRUCTIONS

HOW TO DRAW THE NATIONAL FLAG OF THE REPUBLIC OF SOUTH AFRICA

1. Draw a rectangle in the proportion of 3 in the length to 2 in the height (for example 180 mm x 120 mm).
2. Using a pencil, divide this rectangle into three equal horizontal bands.
3. Join the four corners by means of a diagonal cross.
4. On each side of this diagonal cross, which provides the centre line in each case, draw parallel lines. The distance between each set of lines should be one third of the width of the flag. Join the various lines as shown opposite.
5. Within the Y-shaped area which extends from the corners at the flagpost (the pall) to the outer edge of the fly, draw a series of parallel lines, the distance between being one fifth of the width of the flag. Join the appropriate lines as indicated and erase the remaining pencil lines.
6. Colour the surfaces as shown.

COLOUR SPECIFICATIONS

The colours of the National Flag of the Republic of South Africa, South African Bureau of Standards -

Textile colours:

Green -	CKS 42c	Spectrum green
Black -	CKS 401c	Blue black
White -	CKS 701c	National Flag white
Gold -	CKS 724c	Gold yellow
Red -	CKS 750c	Chilli red
Blue -	CKS 762c	National Flag blue

Pantone colours:

Green -	3415c
Gold -	1235c
Red -	179c
Blue -	Reflex Blue c

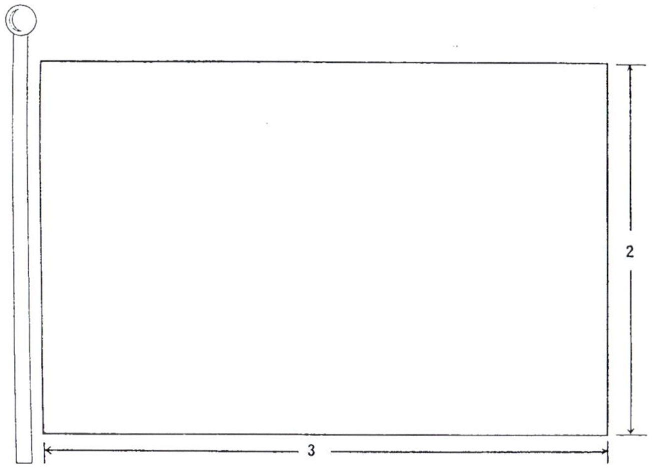

1.

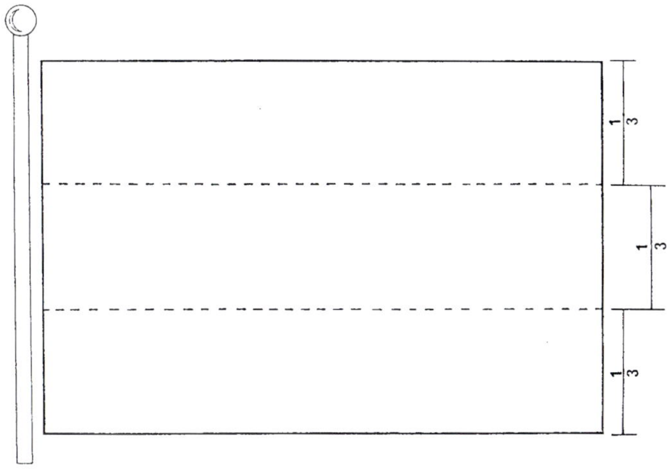

2.

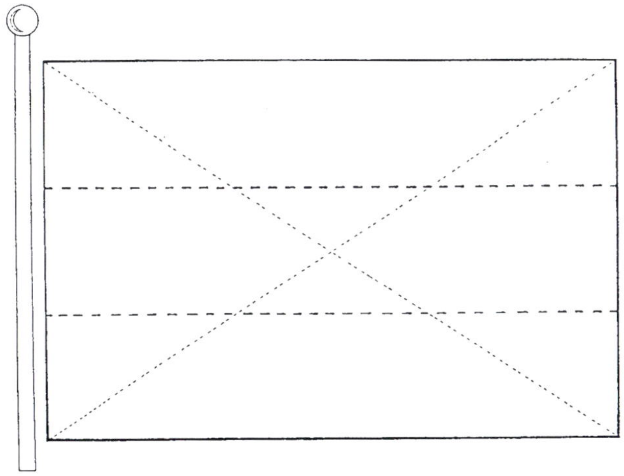

3.

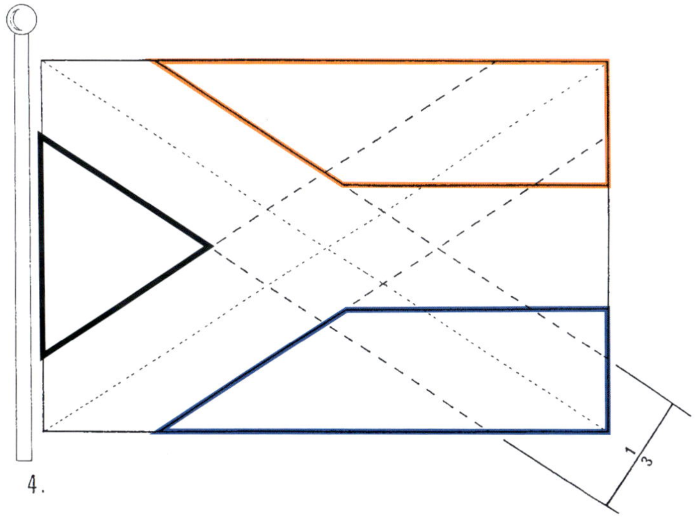

4.

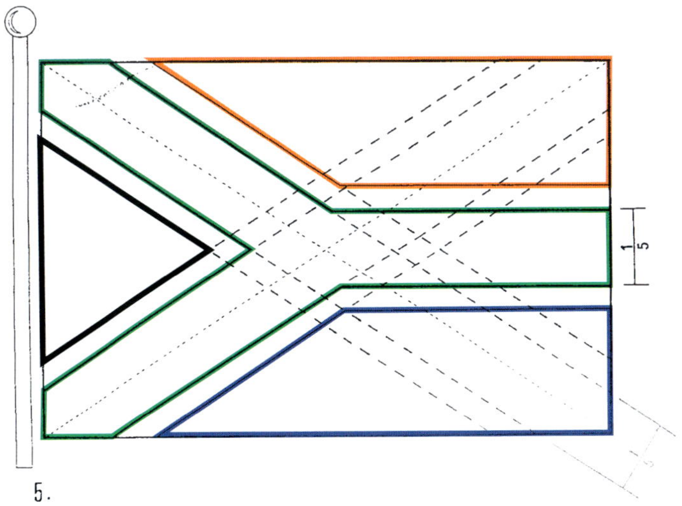

5.

6.

The design and symbolism of the

COAT OF ARMS OF THE REPUBLIC OF SOUTH AFRICA

Information from the Government Communication Information System

The Coat of Arms is a series of elements organised in two distinct circles placed on top of one another.

THE MOTTO – *!ke e: /xarra //ke*, written in the Khosian language of the /Xam people, literally meaning: diverse people unite. It addresses each individual effort to harness the unity between thought and action. On a collective scale it calls for the nation to unite in a common sense of belonging and national pride - Unity in Diversity.

ELEPHANT TUSKS – symbolise wisdom, strength, moderation and eternity.

THE EARS OF WHEAT – in the circle formed by the tusks – symbolise fertility, growth and the development of potential, the nourishment of people and the agricultural aspects of the earth.

THE SHIELD – the shape of the gold shield is drum-like. It has a dual function: the display of identity and of spiritual defence.

THE HUMAN FIGURES – are derived from images on the Linton Stone, a world famous example of South African Rock Art, now housed and displayed in the South African Museum in Cape Town. The Khoisan, the oldest known inhabitants of our land, testify to our common humanity and heritage as South Africans. The figures are depicted in an attitude of greeting, symbolising unity. This also represents the beginning of the individual's transformation into the greater sense of belonging to the nation and by extension, collective Humanity.

THE SPEAR AND KNOBKIERRIE – dual symbols of defence and authority – also represent the powerful legs of the secretary bird. The spear and knobkierrie are lying down, symbolising peace.

THE PROTEA – an emblem of the beauty of our land and the flowering of our potential as a nation in pursuit of the African Renaissance – symbolises the holistic integration of forces that grow from the earth, nurtured from above.

THE SECRETARY BIRD – characterised in flight – the natural consequence of growth and speed. It is a powerful bird whose legs – depicted as the spear and knobkierrie – serve it well in its hunt for snakes symbolising protection of the nation against its enemies. It is a messenger of the heavens and conducts its grace upon the earth, in this sense it is a symbol of divine majesty, Its uplifted wings are an emblem of the ascendance of our nation, whilst simultaneously offering us their protection.

THE RISING SUN – an emblem of brightness and splendour. It symbolises the promise of rebirth, the active faculties of reflection, knowledge, good judgement and willpower. It is the symbol of the source of life, of light and the ultimate wholeness of Humanity.

THE COMPLETED STRUCTURE – the completed structure of the Coat of Arms combines the lower and higher circles in a symbol of infinity. The path that connects the lower edge of the scroll, through the lines of the tusks, with the horizon above which the sun rises at the top, forms the shape of the cosmic egg from which the secretary bird rises. In the symbolic sense this is the implied rebirth of the spirit of our great and heroic nation.

Selected extracts from The South African Government Gazette, 8 June 2001

Government notice

INSTRUCTIONS REGARDING THE FLYING OF THE NATIONAL FLAG OF THE REPUBLIC

DESIGN OF THE NATIONAL FLAG

The design of the National Flag is described in the Schedule to Proclamation no. 70, 1994 as published in Government Gazette no. 15663 of 20 April 1994.

The National Flag shall be rectangular in the proportion of two in the width to three in the length; per pall from the hoist, the upper band chilli red and the lower band blue, with a black triangle at the hoist, over the partition lines a green pall one fifth the width of the flag, fimbriated white against the chilli red and blue, and gold against the black triangle at the hoist; the width of the pall and its fimbriations is one third the width of the flag.

HOISTING OF THE NATIONAL FLAG

Except on ceremonial occasions, where the National Flag should be hoisted unfurled, it should at the specified hour be hoisted rolled-up to break at the truck. At sunset, or at the appointed time, it should be lowered slowly.

HALF-MASTING OF THE NATIONAL FLAG

The National Flag should be half-masted as a sign of mourning only on instructions from The Presidency. When the National Flag is half-masted, it should first be hoisted to the top of the flagstaff and then slowly lowered until the centre of the flag is half way between the truck and the bottom of the flagstaff. Before the flag is lowered at sunset, or at the appointed time, it should first be hoisted to the top of the flagstaff.

GENERAL INSTRUCTIONS

When the National Flag is displayed vertically against a wall, the red band should be to the left of the spectator with the hoist or the cord seam uppermost; when it is displayed horizontally, the hoist should be to the left of the spectator and the red band uppermost.

When the National flag is displayed next to or behind the speaker in a hall or other meeting place, for example with him on stage, it must be placed on the speaker's right hand. When it is placed elsewhere in the hall or meeting place it should be to the right of the audience as they face the speaker.

When the National Flag is displayed together with:

(a) any other flags, it must be hoisted first and lowered last;

(b) the national flags of any other countries, all the flags should be of approximately equal size and must be flown at an equal height, and the National Flag of the Republic of South Africa must be on the right side of the building or platform (that is to say, on the left side from the observer's point of view);

(c) any other flags, not being national flags, on separate flag staffs, the National Flag must be in the middle or on the left side from the observer's point of view or at the highest point of the group;

(d) any other flags on the same flagstaff, it must be at the top;

(e) any other flag on crossed staffs, the National Flag must be to spectator's left and its staff must be in front of the staff of the other flag; and

(f) another flag or flags in procession, the National Flag must be on the marching right (that is to say, on the left side from the observer's point of view). If there is a row of flags, the provisions of (c) above apply.

RESPECT FOR THE NATIONAL FLAG

The National Flag must at all times be treated with dignity and respect. The flag must not:

a) touch the floor or the ground;

b) be used as a tablecloth or be draped in front of a platform;

c) be used to cover a statue, plaque, cornerstone, etc., at unveiling or similar ceremonies; or

d) be used to start or finish any competition, race or similar event.

IMPORTANT CONTACTS

THE PRESIDENCY

For all permissions relating to the use of the flag.

Private Bag X1000

Pretoria

0001

Tel: 012-300-5200

Fax: 012-323-8246

www.gov.za/president

THE DEPARTMENT OF TRADE AND INDUSTRY

For permission to use the flag or its derivation on manufactured products.

Private Bag X274

Pretoria

0001

Tel: 012-322-7677

Tel: 012-310-1376

www.dti.gov.za

THE BUREAU OF HERALDRY

For all matters relating to the flag, national symbols and heraldry.

Private Bag X236

Pretoria

0001

Tel: 012-323-5300

Fax: 012-323-5287

THE DEPARTMENT OF ARTS, CULTURE, SCIENCE AND TECHNOLOGY

The organisers of Freedom Day celebrations, South Africa's official ceremonial day.

Private Bag X727

Pretoria

0001

Tel: 012-337-8000

Tel: 012-323-2720

www.dacst.gov.za

Flags and flag-related products

See **www.FlyingWithPride.co.za**

PHOTOGRAPHIC CREDITS

Cover - Luc Hosten/Gallo Images
page 1 - Gary Bernard/PictureNet
3 - The Star
6 - Franz Rabe/WildNet Africa
13 - Luc Hosten/Gallo Images
15 - Henner Frankenfeld/PictureNet
17 - Harry Said
19 - Sunday Times
20 - Beeld
22 - Sunday Times
25 - Zapiro/Trace Images
27 - Sunday Times
28 - Beeld
30 - Gary Prior/Allsport/Touchline
32 - Sunday Times
33 - Eddie Mtsweni/PictureNet
34 - Independent Newspapers/Trace Images
Independent Newspapers/Trace Images
35 - Sunday Times
Independent Newspapers/Trace Images
36 - Tertius Pickard/Touchline
38 - Tertius Pickard/Touchline
39 - David Rogers/Allsport/Touchline
40 - Dennis Farrell/PictureNet
43 - South African National Archives
45 - from "The Flag and Good Faith"
by Sir Percy Fitzpatrick (pub. Cape Times Limited)
46 - Benny Gool/Trace Images
47 - Raúl Gil
48 - The Star
51 - Adam Welz
52 - Wayne Griffiths/Gallo Images
53 - Wayne Griffiths/Gallo Images
54 - Sasa Kralj/PictureNet
55 - Independent Newspapers/Trace Images
56 - Pretoria News
58 - Beeld
59 - Sunday Times
60 - Don Boroughs/PictureNet
61 - Independent Newspapers/Trace Images
64 - David Guttenfelder/PictureNet
67 - Independent Newspapers/Trace Images
68 - Lauren Dickson
69 - Clive Grinaker/Grinaker Sports Marketing
70 - Peter Ripton
71 - Chris van der Merwe
73 - Franz Rabe/WildNet Africa
76 - Franz Rabe/WildNet Africa
79 - Sunday Times
81 - Gary Bernard/PictureNet
84 - Independent Newspapers/Trace Images
87 - Sunday Times
88 - Sunday Times
91 - Sunday Times
92 - Themba Hadebe/PictureNet
93 - Pretoria News
94 - Sunday Times
95 - Independent Newspapers/Trace Images
96 - Sunday Times
97 - Sunday Times
99 - Sunday Times
100 - Franz Rabe/WildNet Africa
102 - Franz Rabe/WildNet Africa
103 - Eddie Mtsweni/PictureNet
104 - Franz Rabe/WildNet Africa
105 - Andrew Bannister/Gallo Images
106 - Independent Newspapers/Trace Images
107 - Sunday Times
109 - Keith Young/iAfrica
110 - Sunday Times
111 - Sunday Times
112 - Colin Whelan/Touchline
113 - Siddique Davids/PictureNet
114 - Beeld
116 - Independent Newspapers/Trace Images
117 - Duif du Toit/Touchline
118 - Leon Breytenbach
120 - Sunday Times
121 - Keith Young/iAfrica
123 - Franz Rabe/WildNet Africa
124 - Franz Rabe/WildNet Africa
126 - Sunday Times
128 - Sunday Times
129 - South African Airways
130 - Leon Breytenbach
131 - Daimler Chrysler
133 - Tertius Pickard/Touchline
135 - Independent Newspapers/Trace Images
136 - Beeld
138 - Franz Rabe/WildNet Africa
140 - Franz Rabe/WildNet Africa
141 - Frans Dely
143 - Pieter Dirk Uys
144 - Franz Rabe/WildNet Africa
145 - Sasa Kralj/iAfrica
147 - TJ Lemon
148 - Linda Suskin/Viewfinder
149 - Linda Suskin/Viewfinder
152 - The Star
154 - Daryl Balfour/Gallo Images
156 - The Star
157 - Des Steward/iAfrica
158 - Sunday Times